If there is anything holding you back,

or any sacrifice you are afraid of making,

come to God and prove how gracious your God is.

Never be afraid that He will command from you

what He will not bestow! God comes and offers

to work this absolute surrender in you.

Andrew Murray[1]

©2022 *Revive Our Hearts*

Published by *Revive Our Hearts*

P.O. Box 2000, Niles, MI 49120
ISBN: 978-1-934718-88-9

Printed in the United States of America.

All rights reserved. No part of this publication may be reproduced in any form without permission from the publisher, except in the case of brief quotations embodied in other works or reviews.

Adapted from Nancy Leigh DeMoss, *Surrender: The Heart God Controls* (©2005). Published by Moody Publishers. Used by permission.

Additional content provided by Katie Laitkep.

Edited by Erin Davis, Mindy Kroesche, and Mindi Stearns.

Cover design by Austin Collins. Interior design by Lauren Davis.

Scripture quotations marked CSB have been taken from the Christian Standard Bible®, Copyright © 2017 by Holman Bible Publishers. Used by permission. Christian Standard Bible® and CSB® are federally registered trademarks of Holman Bible Publishers.

As I write these words, some of our Christian brothers and sisters in Indonesia are paying an enormous price to follow Christ. In certain villages that have been taken over by militant Muslims, Christians who refuse to convert to Islam are being "allowed" to leave their villages. The cost of that freedom is that they must forsake their homes and everything they own, and they may never again return to their villages. The only way they can stay is if they agree to become Muslims.

Such a price is unfathomable to most of us. We cannot conceive of being required to literally forsake everything for the sake of Christ. Nonetheless, when we consider Christ's call to full surrender, we may wrestle with real fears of what that might mean for us.

"I surrender all . . ."; "Christ is all I need. . . ." The words roll off our lips as we sing them in church. But it's not so easy to choose to place ourselves in a position where we have to find out if He really is all we need. Although we are not likely to find ourselves in the same situation as those Indonesian believers, full surrender to Christ forces us to face the possibility—or the reality—of giving up some of the things we consider most important in life.

Our natural tendency is to hold on tightly, to try to protect and preserve whatever we think we can't live without. We are afraid that if we surrender *everything* to God—our health, our material possessions, our family, our reputation, our career plans, all our rights, our future—He might take us up on it! We have visions of God stripping us of the things we most need or enjoy, or perhaps sending us out to serve Him in the most inhospitable place on the planet.

Many of our fears about relinquishing total control of our lives to God fall into four categories. If I surrender everything to Him, what about . . .

PROVISION—WILL I HAVE WHAT I NEED? What if I lose my job? What if my husband loses his job? Can we afford to have more children? How will we pay for their education? What if God asks us to give our savings to the church or to a needy family? What if God calls us into vocational ministry— how will we be supported? What if the economy goes under— what will happen to our investments? What if my husband dies—will I have enough to live on?

PLEASURE—WILL I BE HAPPY? If I fully surrender to God, will I be miserable? Will I be able to do the things I enjoy? What if He wants me to give up my career . . . or sports . . . or my favorite hobby . . . or my best friend . . . or the foods I really like? Might God make me stay in this unhappy marriage? Will I be fulfilled if I obey Him?

PROTECTION—WILL I (AND THOSE I LOVE) BE SAFE?

What if my child is born with a mental or physical disability? What if someone abuses my children? What if I have an accident leaving me maimed for life? What if I get cancer? What if someone breaks into our house? Might God choose to take my mate or my children? If my child goes to the mission field, will he be safe?

PERSONAL RELATIONSHIPS—WILL MY RELATIONAL NEEDS BE MET?

What if the Lord wants me to be single all my life? How can I live without sex or romance? What if my mate never loves me? What if God doesn't give us children? What if I lose my mate? How can I handle the rejection of my parents? What if my best friend moves away? What if people reject our family because of our commitment to biblical standards?

Overcoming Fear
WITH FAITH

The pages of Scripture are salted with the stories of men and women who risked everything to follow Christ. Sometimes we think of these people as if they were merely lifeless figures in a wax museum; we forget that they were real people who had to deal with real-life issues.

Take Abraham, for example. We think of Abraham as a superhero—a man of towering faith. And he was. Yet he had to face many of the same issues and fears that we struggle with. Over and over again, in order to move forward in his relationship with God, Abraham was called to make a fresh surrender to God. To do so required that he let go, relinquish control, step out on a limb, and trust a God he could not see.

Abraham grew up in a pagan, idolatrous environment where there was absolutely nothing to inspire or nurture faith—no study Bibles, no praise and worship to stream on his cell phone, no churches, no Christian fellowship. When an unseen, unknown God spoke and told Abram (as he was known at the time) to venture out and leave behind everything that was familiar and comfortable, he was faced with a choice: to stay or to go.

In making that choice, Abram had to consider the cost of surrender:

- How will my family's needs be met? (*provision*)
- Will we be happy? (*pleasure*)
- Will we be safe? (*protection*)
- You want my wife and me to leave all our friends and relatives? (*personal relationships*)

The biblical record does not tell us to what extent, if any, Abram wrestled with his decision. All we know is that he went. Genesis 12:1 records God's call to Abram: "Go from your land, your relatives, and your father's house to the land that I will show you." Three verses later we read, "So Abram went, as the LORD had told him" (12:4).

Without further explanation, with no idea where he was going, how he would get there, or what he would do once he got there, Abram risked everything, cast himself into the arms of Providence . . . and went. He chose friendship with God over all human relationships, earthly attachments, and visible security.

"But," you say, "Abraham had a lot to gain—after all, God had promised to give him a fruitful land and more offspring than he could count." Yes, Abraham was the recipient of grand promises. But keep in mind that for more than twenty-five years, he didn't have a shred of visible evidence that God's promises would be fulfilled. Acts 7:5 reminds us of the reality that could easily have shaken Abraham's faith: He had "no inheritance" and "no child." But he went anyway. And, in spite of occasional lapses in his faith, he kept going.

Abraham surrendered himself to the purposes and plans of God, with no tangible guarantee that his obedience would ever "pay off." Even when he could not see the outcome of his faith, he believed God. He staked his life, his security, his future—everything—on the fact that God was real and that He would keep His promises (Heb. 11:6). That was the foundation on which his faith rested. That was what motivated his repeated acts of surrender.

> Abraham staked his life, his security, his future—EVERYTHING—on the fact that God was real and that He would keep His promises.

It was faith in the character and the promises of God that enabled Abraham and his wife, Sarah, to embrace an itinerant lifestyle—living in tents—for more than twenty-five years.

It was faith in the promises of God that sustained the couple through decades of infertility and unfulfilled longings.

It was faith in the promises of God that motivated Abram to surrender the best land option to his nephew Lot and to trust that God would provide a suitable inheritance for him (Gen. 13:1–11).

It was the character and the promises of God that gave Abram courage (at the age of seventy-five!) to take on the massive military machine of the allied kings of the East, in order to rescue his errant nephew (Gen. 14).

When Abram was tempted to fear reprisals from the defeated kings, God bolstered his faith with a rehearsal of His promises: "Do not be afraid, Abram. I am your shield; your reward will be very great" (Gen. 15:1). What was God saying? *I am your protection and your provision; if you have Me, you have all you need. So . . . trust Me!*

At times, the call of God in our lives may require us to relinquish things or people we can't imagine living without—material possessions, a job or a promotion, good health, a mate or a child, or the respect and understanding of our closest friends. The promises of God provide a powerful antidote to all our fears and free us to step out in faith and surrender.

Stranger on Earth
FRIEND OF GOD

Abram came to be known by his contemporaries as "Abram the Hebrew" (Gen. 14:13). The word *Hebrew* means "stranger" or "alien." From earth's perspective, he was always something of a "misfit"; he didn't really belong. But that was okay. He understood that everything this world offers is temporary at best. His ultimate citizenship wasn't on this earth. He was living for an eternal home (Heb. 11:16). He was willing to venture everything this world considers vital—homeland, reputation, position, possessions, family, prestige—in order to be eternally secure and to gain the blessing of God. And that is exactly what happened.

Though he was an alien on earth, from heaven's perspective Abraham was called the "friend of God" (James 2:23). The development of this man's extraordinary relationship with God can be defined in terms of a series of surrenders made over a lifetime. Each of those surrenders was based on a revelation of the promise-making, promise-keeping God.

Altars
OF SURRENDER

Perhaps the most appropriate symbol of Abraham's life is an altar. On four distinct occasions, at different stages in his pilgrimage, we are told that Abraham responded to God by building an altar. First at Shechem (Gen. 12:7), then between Bethel and Ai (12:8), then at Hebron (13:18), Abraham erected altars—silent symbols of surrender and faith.

Then, on a mountain named Moriah, the man who was called the "friend of God" built yet another altar (22:9). On that altar, at God's unmistakable but incomprehensible direction, Abraham placed his own son. It was the ultimate act of surrender—a relinquishing of all he held dear.

In an act not unlike a resurrection, God spared Abraham's son. The test had been passed. God knew that when Abraham laid his precious, long-promised son on the altar and prepared to plunge the knife into his heart, Abraham himself was on the altar—all that he was and all that he had were God's.

All those earlier altars had been preparing Abraham for the moment when he would be called upon to make a supreme sacrifice. With each act of surrender, the trustworthiness of God and His promises had been established in Abraham's heart. Likewise, each "small" step of surrender that we take confirms that God is worthy of our trust and prepares us to trust Him with bigger surrenders that may be required down the road.

> Each "small" step of surrender that we take confirms that GOD IS WORTHY OF OUR TRUST and prepares us to trust Him with bigger surrenders that may be required down the road.

Altars speak of sacrifice and devotion—of being consumed. They speak of a life that is wholly given up to the one for whom the altar is built. Many churches identify a location or an object at the front of the sanctuary as an "altar." Though we don't light fires and offer literal sacrifices on those sites, they are intended to serve as visible reminders of what ought to be a spiritual reality for every child of God—as the hymn writer put it, "My heart an altar, and Thy love the flame."[2]

Promises THAT COUNTER OUR FEARS

The surrender points Abraham faced over the course of his life may be similar to some you have faced: leaving family and friends behind and moving to a new city where you didn't know a soul ... making choices to sacrifice your own interests for the sake of others ... staying engaged with and pursuing the heart of a rebellious relative ... living with infertility ... turning down a lucrative offer that you know is not pleasing to God ... giving up the life of a child.

When it comes to the uncertainties that keep us from sacrifice, surrender, and submission to God, we, like Abraham, have exceedingly "great and precious promises" (2 Pet. 1:4) from God's Word—promises that powerfully counteract our deepest fears. If we trust those promises and the God who has made them, we will be given courage to make each sacrifice He asks of us.

If we do not trust God's promises and, therefore, do not step out in faith and surrender, we will ultimately find ourselves in bondage to the very things we refuse to surrender. We will end up being controlled by that which we are seeking to keep within our own control.

Trust or tyranny. That is the option. *Trust* the promises of God—which will free you to live joyfully under His loving lordship—or live under the *tyranny* of that which you will not surrender.

God wants us to experience provision, pleasure, protection, and personal relationships. But He wants us to seek them in the only place they can be found—in Him. And He doesn't want us to settle for substitutes for the real thing.

Provision. Scripture exhorts us to be content with what we have (Heb. 13:5) and not to worry about how our future needs will be met (Matt. 6:25–34). The basis for contentment and freedom from anxiety is that God has promised to provide all that we need (though not necessarily all that we want) (Phil. 4:19). Based on His promise, when we have a need, rather than fretting, striving, or manipulating, we ought to simply and confidently ask Him to provide (Matt. 7:7; Phil. 4:6).

If we are unwilling to trust God in the matter of provision, we may be tyrannized by greed, stealing, cheating, lack of generosity, lying, worrying, coveting, or centering our lives around money.

Pleasure. We cannot escape the fact that pain is unavoidable in this fallen world and that suffering is an instrument that God uses to mold and sanctify those He loves. But God also created us to experience intense pleasure and joy. The problem is that we are prone to seek pleasure in things and people that cannot ultimately satisfy the deep longing in our hearts. For our hearts can never be truly satisfied apart from Him. The unsurrendered heart pursues what are paltry pleasures compared with the pure, infinite pleasures God wants to give us:

> In the midst of our earthly journey, the joy Christ offers lifts us beyond our circumstances and provides us with a breathtaking foretaste of heaven's eternal pleasures.

You reveal the path of life to me;
in your presence is abundant joy;
at your right hand are eternal pleasures.

How priceless your faithful love is, God!
People take refuge in the shadow of your wings.

> *They are filled from the abundance of your house.*
> *You let them drink from your refreshing stream.*
> —Psalm 16:11, 36:7–8

Even fully surrendered saints sometimes experience sorrow, suffering, and struggles. But in the midst of our earthly journey, the joy Christ offers lifts us beyond our circumstances and provides us with a breathtaking foretaste of heaven's eternal pleasures.

However, if we are unwilling to trust God with our happiness and well-being, and we insist on the pursuit of temporal pleasures, we may become dominated by overeating, getting drunk or using drugs, sexual promiscuity, adultery, pornography, obsession with television or films or novels, being irresponsible, or living beyond our means.

Protection. Our God is a refuge, a fortress, a shelter, and a strong deliverer to His children. Psalm 91 speaks of God's amazing protection:

> *I will say concerning the LORD, who is my refuge and my fortress,*
> *my God in whom I trust:*
> *He himself will rescue you from the bird trap,*
> *from the destructive plague.*
> *He will cover you with his feathers;*
> *you will take refuge under his wings.*

> *His faithfulness will be a protective shield.*
> *You will not fear the terror of the night,*
> *the arrow that flies by day,*
> *the plague that stalks in darkness,*
> *or the pestilence that ravages at noon.* —Psalm 91:2–6

God doesn't promise that we will never face danger, but those who take refuge in Him are placed under His protection. He assures us that He will defend us and keep us free from fear, no matter what comes our way.

However, if we do not entrust our safety to God, but demand human assurance of protection and security, we may be overwhelmed by fearfulness, worry, mistrust of people, obsession with weapons, unwillingness to be vulnerable, fear of intimacy, tendencies toward violence, hatred, prejudice, conspiracy theories, or paranoid-type thoughts.

Personal relationships. It is true that God may lead us into solitude for a season. But His Word makes it clear that an intimate relationship with Him is the basis for the richest of human relationships (1 John 1:3, 7). God Himself has promised to remain with us, to be our constant companion, wherever we go, whatever we do. "I will never leave you or abandon you," He has vowed (Heb. 13:5).

Throughout the Scripture, whenever one of His children was fearful to step out alone, without human support, God's simple response was, *I will be with you.* The implication was—*I am enough. If you have Me, you have everything you need.*

The man or woman who trusts His promises can say with the psalmist,

> *Who do I have in heaven but you?*
> *And I desire nothing on earth but you.* —Psalm 73:25

If we do not value *Him* as our primary relationship, we will live in fear of losing human relationships and will set ourselves up to be tyrannized by such things as possessiveness, giving or taking abuse, adultery, promiscuity, gossip, possessive or controlling relationships, lust, dissatisfaction, unforgiveness, bitterness, manipulation, dishonesty, or jealousy.

Things We Can Count On

Ann Blocher was first diagnosed with breast cancer in 1977, when her five children were young adults. After going through chemotherapy, she went into apparent remission. Several years later, the cancer reappeared. After battling to control the cancer with chemo and diet, she finally went home to be with the Lord in 1986.

As she walked through those tempestuous and uncertain years, Ann had to face numerous fears about her future and her family. One of the things she struggled with was her desire to be a part of her children's lives. As she dealt with each issue, Ann discovered that the surrender God was asking of her really came down to a matter of trust. She expressed that perspective in a poem written less than three years before her homegoing:

Yes, Lord!
YES AND AMEN!

Can you trust Me, child?
Not only for ultimate eternity,
of which you know next to nothing,
and so are not tempted to meddle—
But for the little span of your life between
the Now and Then, where you envision
decline and separations and failures,
impairments, pain, bereavements, disappointments—
Do you find Me qualified to be Lord of your last days?
Oh—yes, Lord! YES, Lord! Yes and amen!

Can you trust Me, child?
Not only to synchronize the unthinkable
intricacies of creation—
But to work together for good the gravities
and tugs within your little orbit,

> where your heart is pulled by needs
> and lacks you wish, but are destitute, to fill—
> Do you find My resources adequate
> to feed both the sparrows and you?
> Oh—yes, Lord! YES, Lord! Yes and amen!
>
> Can you trust Me, child?
> Not only for the oversight of nations
> and creations not of this world—
> But for those beloved ones I committed
> to you and you committed to Me—
> Do you believe Me trustworthy to perform
> the good work begun in them
> until the Day of Jesus Christ?
> Oh—yes, Lord! YES, Lord! Yes and amen![3]

As Ann Blocher cast herself upon the character, the heart, and the promises of God, she was enabled to respond to the will of God in wholehearted surrender—whether that meant being sick or well, living or dying.

Isn't that the heart of the matter for every child of God? Can you trust Me?

Whatever your fears, whatever the unknowns or the challenges in your life, God has promised to provide for you, to share His pleasure with you, to protect you, and to give you His enduring presence.

The fact remains that when we sign the blank contract of surrender, there are no guarantees about where God will lead us or how difficult our journey will be. Yet we know the character of the One in whom we've placed our trust. And we know that God's promises more than offset any risks or dangers or challenges that He may allow into our lives.

Making It Personal

Which of the four fears identified in this chapter do you most relate to?

_____
_____
_____
_____
_____
_____
_____
_____
_____
_____
_____

How has that fear caused you to hold back from surrendering some part of your life to God?

_____
_____
_____
_____
_____
_____
_____
_____
_____
_____

What is one promise in God's Word that addresses your fear?

_____
_____
_____
_____
_____
_____
_____
_____
_____

SCRIPTURE TO COUNTER YOUR FEARS

Scripture to Pray
WHEN YOU ARE FEELING AFRAID ABOUT . . .

1. Death
2. Financial Instability
3. An Uncertain Diagnosis
4. Becoming a Parent
5. Natural Disasters
6. Failure
7. Children Rebelling Against God
8. War and Civil Unrest
9. A Spouse Being Unfaithful
10. Growing Older
11. Infertility
12. Facing Persecution
13. Being Known
14. Remaining Single
15. The Future

How to Pray Scripture
WHEN YOU FEEL AFRAID

How do you quiet your heart when you feel afraid? **Throughout history, followers of Christ have found refuge in the book of Psalms.** This collection of prayers was preserved to help God's people communicate with Him in the midst of life's crises and confusion.

When the psalmists recorded their prayers to the Lord, they experienced different circumstances than ones you face today. Times may have changed since these words were first written, but God has not. The Psalms capture the Lord's unwavering character and His ability to provide for you, protect you, and give you His enduring presence.

When you feel worried about challenges you're facing, the Psalms provide language from God that you can speak back to Him. As you begin praying through them,

- Ask God to quiet your heart and speak to you through His Word.
- Read each line slowly, paying close attention to descriptions of God.
    - What is He like?
    - In what ways is He shown to be trustworthy?

- Meditate on the truth about God, and consider how it applies to your own situation.
- Follow the psalmist's lead in praising God and placing your hope in Him.
- Consider reading through the psalm out loud or rereading meaningful parts.
- Take one thought away: write down one phrase or verse from the psalm that will remind you of God's faithfulness in the midst of your fear.

Psalms to Pray
WHEN YOU ARE FEARFUL ABOUT...

1. **DEATH**

    Psalm 23

    The Lord is my shepherd;
    I have what I need.
    He lets me lie down in green pastures;
    he leads me beside quiet waters.
    He renews my life;
    he leads me along the right paths
    for his name's sake.
    Even when I go through the darkest valley,

I fear no danger,
for you are with me;
your rod and your staff—they comfort me.

You prepare a table before me
in the presence of my enemies;
you anoint my head with oil;
my cup overflows.
Only goodness and faithful love will pursue me
all the days of my life,
and I will dwell in the house of the Lord
as long as I live.

2. FINANCIAL INSTABILITY
Psalm 147

Hallelujah!
How good it is to sing to our God,
for praise is pleasant and lovely.

The Lord rebuilds Jerusalem;
he gathers Israel's exiled people.
He heals the brokenhearted
and bandages their wounds.
He counts the number of the stars;
he gives names to all of them.
Our Lord is great, vast in power;

his understanding is infinite.
The LORD helps the oppressed
but brings the wicked to the ground.

Sing to the LORD with thanksgiving;
play the lyre to our God,
who covers the sky with clouds,
prepares rain for the earth,
and causes grass to grow on the hills.
He provides the animals with their food,
and the young ravens what they cry for.

He is not impressed by the strength of a horse;
he does not value the power of a warrior.
The LORD values those who fear him,
those who put their hope in his faithful love.

Exalt the LORD, Jerusalem;
praise your God, Zion!
For he strengthens the bars of your city gates
and blesses your children within you.
He endows your territory with prosperity;
he satisfies you with the finest wheat.

He sends his command throughout the earth;
his word runs swiftly.
He spreads snow like wool;

he scatters frost like ashes;
he throws his hailstones like crumbs.
Who can withstand his cold?
He sends his word and melts them;
he unleashes his winds, and the water flows.

He declares his word to Jacob,
his statutes and judgments to Israel.
He has not done this for every nation;
they do not know his judgments.
Hallelujah!

3. AN UNCERTAIN DIAGNOSIS
Psalm 13

How long, Lord? Will you forget me forever?
How long will you hide your face from me?
How long will I store up anxious concerns within me,
agony in my mind every day?
How long will my enemy dominate me?

Consider me and answer, Lord my God.
Restore brightness to my eyes;
otherwise, I will sleep in death.

My enemy will say, "I have triumphed over him,"
and my foes will rejoice because I am shaken.

But I have trusted in your faithful love;
my heart will rejoice in your deliverance.
I will sing to the Lord
because he has treated me generously.

4. BECOMING A PARENT
Psalm 144

Blessed be the Lord, my rock
who trains my hands for battle
and my fingers for warfare.
He is my faithful love and my fortress,
my stronghold and my deliverer.
He is my shield, and I take refuge in him;
he subdues my people under me.

Lord, what is a human that you care for him,
a son of man that you think of him?
A human is like a breath;
his days are like a passing shadow.

Lord, part your heavens and come down.
Touch the mountains, and they will smoke.
Flash your lightning and scatter the foe;
shoot your arrows and rout them.
Reach down from on high;
rescue me from deep water, and set me free
from the grasp of foreigners
whose mouths speak lies,
whose right hands are deceptive.

God, I will sing a new song to you;
I will play on a ten-stringed harp for you—
the one who gives victory to kings,
who frees his servant David
from the deadly sword.
Set me free and rescue me
from foreigners
whose mouths speak lies,
whose right hands are deceptive.

Then our sons will be like plants
nurtured in their youth,
our daughters, like corner pillars
that are carved in the palace style.
Our storehouses will be full,
supplying all kinds of produce;
our flocks will increase by thousands

and tens of thousands in our open fields.
Our cattle will be well fed.
There will be no breach in the walls,
no going into captivity,
and no cry of lament in our public squares.
Happy are the people with such blessings.
Happy are the people whose God is the Lord.

5. NATURAL DISASTERS
Psalm 46

God is our refuge and strength,
a helper who is always found
in times of trouble.
Therefore we will not be afraid,
though the earth trembles
and the mountains topple
into the depths of the seas,
though its water roars and foams
and the mountains quake with its turmoil. *Selah*

There is a river—
its streams delight the city of God,
the holy dwelling place of the Most High.
God is within her; she will not be toppled.
God will help her when the morning dawns.
Nations rage, kingdoms topple;

the earth melts when he lifts his voice.
The LORD of Armies is with us;
the God of Jacob is our stronghold. *Selah*

Come, see the works of the LORD
who brings devastation on the earth.
He makes wars cease throughout the earth.
He shatters bows and cuts spears to pieces;
he sets wagons ablaze.
"Stop fighting, and know that I am God,
exalted among the nations, exalted on the earth."
The LORD of Armies is with us;
the God of Jacob is our stronghold. *Selah*

6. FAILURE

Psalm 127

Unless the LORD builds a house,
its builders labor over it in vain;
unless the LORD watches over a city,
the watchman stays alert in vain.
In vain you get up early and stay up late,
working hard to have enough food—
yes, he gives sleep to the one he loves.

Sons are indeed a heritage from the LORD,
offspring, a reward.
Like arrows in the hand of a warrior
are the sons born in one's youth.
Happy is the man who has filled his quiver with them.
They will never be put to shame
when they speak with their enemies at the city gate.

7. CHILDREN REBELLING AGAINST GOD
Psalm 27

The LORD is my light and my salvation—
whom should I fear?
The LORD is the stronghold of my life—
whom should I dread?
When evildoers came against me to devour my flesh,
my foes and my enemies stumbled and fell.
Though an army deploys against me,
my heart will not be afraid;
though a war breaks out against me,
I will still be confident.

I have asked one thing from the LORD;
it is what I desire:

to dwell in the house of the Lord
all the days of my life,
gazing on the beauty of the Lord
and seeking him in his temple.
For he will conceal me in his shelter
in the day of adversity;
he will hide me under the cover of his tent;
he will set me high on a rock.
Then my head will be high
above my enemies around me;
I will offer sacrifices in his tent with shouts of joy.
I will sing and make music to the Lord.

Lord, hear my voice when I call;
be gracious to me and answer me.
My heart says this about you:
"Seek his face."
Lord, I will seek your face.
Do not hide your face from me;
do not turn your servant away in anger.
You have been my helper;
do not leave me or abandon me,
God of my salvation.
Even if my father and mother abandon me,
the Lord cares for me.

Because of my adversaries,
show me your way, Lord,
and lead me on a level path.
Do not give me over to the will of my foes,
for false witnesses rise up against me,
breathing violence.

I am certain that I will see the Lord's goodness
in the land of the living.
Wait for the Lord;
be strong, and let your heart be courageous.
Wait for the Lord.

8. WAR AND CIVIL UNREST
Psalm 3

Lord, how my foes increase!
There are many who attack me.
Many say about me,
"There is no help for him in God." *Selah*

But you, Lord, are a shield around me,
my glory, and the one who lifts up my head.
I cry aloud to the Lord,
and he answers me from his holy mountain. *Selah*

I lie down and sleep;
I wake again because the Lord sustains me.
I will not be afraid of thousands of people
who have taken their stand against me on every side

Rise up, Lord!
Save me, my God!
You strike all my enemies on the cheek;
you break the teeth of the wicked.
Salvation belongs to the Lord;
may your blessing be on your people. *Selah*

9. A SPOUSE BEING UNFAITHFUL
Psalm 62

I am at rest in God alone;
my salvation comes from him.
He alone is my rock and my salvation,
my stronghold; I will never be shaken.

How long will you threaten a man?
Will all of you attack
as if he were a leaning wall
or a tottering fence?

They only plan to bring him down
from his high position.
They take pleasure in lying;
they bless with their mouths,
but they curse inwardly. *Selah*

Rest in God alone, my soul,
for my hope comes from him.
He alone is my rock and my salvation,
my stronghold; I will not be shaken.
My salvation and glory depend on God, my strong rock.
My refuge is in God.
Trust in him at all times, you people;
pour out your hearts before him.
God is our refuge. *Selah*

Common people are only a vapor;
important people, an illusion.
Together on a scale,
they weigh less than a vapor.
Place no trust in oppression
or false hope in robbery.
If wealth increases,
don't set your heart on it.

God has spoken once;
I have heard this twice:

strength belongs to God,
and faithful love belongs to you, Lord.
For you repay each according to his works.

10. GROWING OLDER

Psalm 92

It is good to give thanks to the LORD,
to sing praise to your name, Most High,
to declare your faithful love in the morning
and your faithfulness at night,
with a ten-stringed harp
and the music of a lyre.

For you have made me rejoice, LORD,
by what you have done;
I will shout for joy
because of the works of your hands.
How magnificent are your works, LORD,
how profound your thoughts!
A stupid person does not know,
a fool does not understand this:
though the wicked sprout like grass
and all evildoers flourish,

they will be eternally destroyed.
But you, Lord, are exalted forever.
For indeed, Lord, your enemies—
indeed, your enemies will perish;
all evildoers will be scattered.
You have lifted up my horn
like that of a wild ox;
I have been anointed with the finest oil.
My eyes look at my enemies;
when evildoers rise against me,
my ears hear them.

The righteous thrive like a palm tree
and grow like a cedar tree in Lebanon.
Planted in the house of the Lord,
they thrive in the courts of our God.
They will still bear fruit in old age,
healthy and green,
to declare, "The Lord is just;
he is my rock,
and there is no unrighteousness in him."

11. INFERTILITY

Psalm 16

Protect me, God, for I take refuge in you.
I said to the Lord, "You are my Lord;
I have nothing good besides you."
As for the holy people who are in the land,
they are the noble ones.
All my delight is in them.
The sorrows of those who take another god
for themselves will multiply;
I will not pour out their drink offerings of blood,
and I will not speak their names with my lips.

Lord, you are my portion
and my cup of blessing;
you hold my future.
The boundary lines have fallen for me
in pleasant places;
indeed, I have a beautiful inheritance.

I will bless the Lord who counsels me—
even at night when my thoughts trouble me.
I always let the Lord guide me.
Because he is at my right hand,
I will not be shaken.

Therefore my heart is glad
and my whole being rejoices;
my body also rests securely.
For you will not abandon me to Sheol;
you will not allow your faithful one to see decay.
You reveal the path of life to me;
in your presence is abundant joy;
at your right hand are eternal pleasures.

12. FACING PERSECUTION
Psalm 118

Give thanks to the LORD, for he is good;
his faithful love endures forever.
Let Israel say,
"His faithful love endures forever."
Let the house of Aaron say,
"His faithful love endures forever."
Let those who fear the LORD say,
"His faithful love endures forever."

I called to the LORD in distress;
the LORD answered me
and put me in a spacious place.

The Lord is for me; I will not be afraid.
What can a mere mortal do to me?
The Lord is my helper;
therefore, I will look in triumph on those who hate me.

It is better to take refuge in the Lord
than to trust in humanity.
It is better to take refuge in the Lord
than to trust in nobles.

All the nations surrounded me;
in the name of the Lord I destroyed them.
They surrounded me, yes, they surrounded me;
in the name of the Lord I destroyed them.
They surrounded me like bees;
they were extinguished like a fire among thorns;
in the name of the Lord I destroyed them.
They pushed me hard to make me fall,
but the Lord helped me.
The Lord is my strength and my song;
he has become my salvation.

There are shouts of joy and victory
in the tents of the righteous:
"The Lord's right hand performs valiantly!
The Lord's right hand is raised.
The Lord's right hand performs valiantly!"

I will not die, but I will live
and proclaim what the Lord has done.
The Lord disciplined me severely
but did not give me over to death.

Open the gates of righteousness for me;
I will enter through them
and give thanks to the Lord.
This is the Lord's gate;
the righteous will enter through it.
I will give thanks to you
because you have answered me
and have become my salvation.
The stone that the builders rejected
has become the cornerstone.
This came from the Lord;
it is wondrous in our sight.
This is the day the Lord has made;
let's rejoice and be glad in it.

Lord, save us!
Lord, please grant us success!
He who comes in the name
of the Lord is blessed.
From the house of the Lord we bless you.
The Lord is God and has given us light.
Bind the festival sacrifice with cords

to the horns of the altar.
You are my God, and I will give you thanks.
You are my God; I will exalt you.
Give thanks to the LORD, for he is good;
his faithful love endures forever.

13. BEING KNOWN

Psalm 139

LORD, you have searched me and known me.
You know when I sit down and when I stand up;
you understand my thoughts from far away.
You observe my travels and my rest;
you are aware of all my ways.
Before a word is on my tongue,
you know all about it, LORD.
You have encircled me;
you have placed your hand on me.
This wondrous knowledge is beyond me.
It is lofty; I am unable to reach it.

Where can I go to escape your Spirit?
Where can I flee from your presence?
If I go up to heaven, you are there;

if I make my bed in Sheol, you are there.
If I fly on the wings of the dawn
and settle down on the western horizon,
even there your hand will lead me;
your right hand will hold on to me.
If I say, "Surely the darkness will hide me,
and the light around me will be night"—
even the darkness is not dark to you.
The night shines like the day;
darkness and light are alike to you.

For it was you who created my inward parts;
you knit me together in my mother's womb.
I will praise you
because I have been remarkably and wondrously made.
Your works are wondrous,
and I know this very well.
My bones were not hidden from you
when I was made in secret,
when I was formed in the depths of the earth.
Your eyes saw me when I was formless;
all my days were written in your book and planned
before a single one of them began.

God, how precious your thoughts are to me;
how vast their sum is!
If I counted them,

they would outnumber the grains of sand;
when I wake up, I am still with you.

God, if only you would kill the wicked—
you bloodthirsty men, stay away from me—
who invoke you deceitfully.
Your enemies swear by you falsely.
Lord, don't I hate those who hate you,
and detest those who rebel against you?
I hate them with extreme hatred;
I consider them my enemies.

Search me, God, and know my heart;
test me and know my concerns.
See if there is any offensive way in me;
lead me in the everlasting way.

14. REMAINING SINGLE
Psalm 33

Rejoice in the Lord, you righteous ones;
praise from the upright is beautiful.
Praise the Lord with the lyre;
make music to him with a ten-stringed harp.
Sing a new song to him;
play skillfully on the strings, with a joyful shout.

For the word of the Lord is right,
and all his work is trustworthy.
He loves righteousness and justice;
the earth is full of the Lord's unfailing love.

The heavens were made by the word of the Lord,
and all the stars, by the breath of his mouth.
He gathers the water of the sea into a heap;
he puts the depths into storehouses.
Let the whole earth fear the Lord;
let all the inhabitants of the world stand in awe of him.
For he spoke, and it came into being;
he commanded, and it came into existence.

The Lord frustrates the counsel of the nations;
he thwarts the plans of the peoples.
The counsel of the Lord stands forever,
the plans of his heart from generation to generation.
Happy is the nation whose God is the Lord—
the people he has chosen to be his own possession!

The Lord looks down from heaven;
he observes everyone.
He gazes on all the inhabitants of the earth
from his dwelling place.
He forms the hearts of them all;
he considers all their works.

A king is not saved by a large army;
a warrior will not be rescued by great strength.
The horse is a false hope for safety;
it provides no escape by its great power.

But look, the LORD keeps his eye on those who fear him—
those who depend on his faithful love
to rescue them from death
and to keep them alive in famine.

We wait for the LORD;
he is our help and shield.
For our hearts rejoice in him
because we trust in his holy name.
May your faithful love rest on us, LORD,
for we put our hope in you.

15. THE FUTURE

Psalm 29

Ascribe to the LORD, you heavenly beings,
ascribe to the LORD glory and strength.
Ascribe to the LORD the glory due his name;
worship the LORD

in the splendor of his holiness.
The voice of the LORD is above the waters.
The God of glory thunders—
the LORD, above the vast water,
the voice of the LORD in power,
the voice of the LORD in splendor.
The voice of the LORD breaks the cedars;
the LORD shatters the cedars of Lebanon.
He makes Lebanon skip like a calf,
and Sirion, like a young wild ox.
The voice of the LORD flashes flames of fire.
The voice of the LORD shakes the wilderness;
the LORD shakes the wilderness of Kadesh.
The voice of the LORD makes the deer give birth
and strips the woodlands bare.
In his temple all cry, "Glory!"

The LORD sits enthroned over the flood;
the LORD sits enthroned, King forever.
The LORD gives his people strength;
the LORD blesses his people with peace.

NOTES

[1] Andrew Murray, *The Believer's Absolute Surrender* (Minneapolis: Bethany, 1985), 78.

[2] George Croly, "Spirit of God, Descend upon my Heart."

[3] Permission for use granted by Betty and Clarence Blocher.

Revive Our Hearts

PRESENTS THE
Women of the Bibl[e]
SERIES

ABIGAIL

Study God's Wo[rd]

Examine the lives of ordinary wor[men]
that point to an extraordinary G[od]

Discover that every s[tory]
is really God's st[ory]

REVIVEOURHEARTS.COM/WOMENOFTHEBIB[LE]

MORE FROM

Revive Our Hearts

RADIO • EVENTS • BLOGS
LEADERS

REVIVE OUR **HEARTS** . COM